IRL

IRL
tommy pico

BIRDS, LLC | MINNEAPOLIS, NEW YORK, RALEIGH

Birds, LLC
Austin, Minneapolis, New York, Raleigh
www.birdsllc.com

Cover designed by Cat Glennon
Interior designed by Michael Newton and Cat Glennon

Cover Image: Marco Polo
© 2016 Cat Glennon

Library of Congress Cataloging-in-Publication Data:
Pico, Tommy
IRL/Tommy Pico
Library of Congress Control Number: 2016941993

First Edition, 2016
ISBN-13: 9780991429868
Printed in the United States of America

I text Girard *do*
u wanna come
over? Watch me stuff
swim trunks into
a weekender bag
and maybe a movie?
Regret is a gift
that keeps on giving I
think it was Sontag
or Sonic the Hedgehog
who said just dash dodge
weave faster than you
can think n there's no
time to shame spiral
Crushing
on Muse—whose
even slight squint bursts
me into high July—
while dialing,
essentially, a trick.
This is my argument:
Muse crashes into
the edges of my nights,
isn't crushing,
doesn't love me,
doesn't have his shit
together (tho neither,
frankly, do I) but yanks
me n my hand onto the dance
floor til tilt-a-whirl Goes on
like land, just accum-
ulating in my eyes.
Girard is a grown ass
man, sly winks
Snakes free drinks
from the bar because

he can pay for the
expensive ones, all
calm n body n blue, and
all Muse and I do
is wander from party
to party, pop off w/ Popov
or Georgi or Poland
Spring Whatever
is deeper than well
and gives you a hang-
over just riding
the subway home.
Lavender candle,
string lights, sage
sticks gathered by my
brother from the rez
to smudge my new
apartment—staging,
I've learned, can be just
as important as what
you whisper into
Girard's ear when
you set the Espelón
down on the end
table beside him
and blow a little
and back away slow,
locked eyes. My room-
mate Jess is a singer/
social worker going
on tour next week,
Danny's in Baltimore,
Deegs visiting parents
So I'll have our four br
apt all to myself when
I get back from the Ham-

ptons. Today a roach
died under my keyboard.
When I sat down
to play, I saw a leaf
and bent to pick
it up. I touched the stem
but it was antennae
and I screamed
bloody murder
and Jess ran in
with a napkin, scooped
it up to heaven. She's
in the other room
humming "We Found
Love in a Hopeless
Place" Struts in
every ten minutes
Asks my opinion of
the design of the
t-shirt she's making
for her tour—higher low-
er bigger smaller left
or right etc.—then
does the exact
opposite of what I suggest.
I'm like, *why even ask?*
She blank blinks,
stands there for
a second drag
from her cig and
walks back to
her room. Ten
minutes later
she busts back
in, asks do
I like where she

wrote the band's name?
I blank blink, stand
there a second, look
down to the swimming
trunks/half-crammed week-
ender bag. She
laughs, says *touché*.
Girard is not coming
over, which almost
makes me mad
But he says *sorry*,
says he wishes he
hadn't made plans
Wishes he could be
with me, and the
phrase "be with"
is a deference
to a kind of growing
infection
I mean affection inside
him that is not
growing inside me, so I
don't respond. If he
said "I'll fuck you
Tuesday" I would
have :-) :-) :-) If
Muse ever texted me
I would :-) :-) :-) If
Muse texted "I
want to be with you"
I would have a
minor coronary incident,
would have to dic-
tate this from Woodhull
Medical Center as I
surely would have

passed head-
first into the evening's
net of basket of
hammer
of stars.
There's my body,
and then there's your body—
basically the plot
of every Beyoncé song
don't write heavenly body
don't write heavenly body
don't write heavenly
Let's call Muse a *heavenly*
body, in the sense that I can't
even think about it—
embodiment of abstract
concept—comedy,
history, bag of salt
& vinegar chips, stellar dimples,
his palm on the support
beam behind you, beside
your hip and leans in
The flood of his breath
the stuff of myths.
Girard has scooped
shoulders in a way that's
easy to clock. In
an effort to protect
the heart, shoulders
pull forward. I sit scooped
shoulders at the computer. Jess
walks in again or doesn't
I can't tell bc I'm horrified
at the Internet, like alcoholism—
oppressive and consuming
occupier god Plus

friends posting about
suicide. Not like famous
suicides or like Wilkes,
who says when the world
goes to shit
she's going She and her Cat
Chairman Meow are going
head first into the oven,
which is romantic. No, like
actually committing suicide
Like Darren in 7th grade
with motor oil or my uncle
Stoney with a shotgun
or Geo and Beam and Guadalupe
three siblings each shook
from life in diff car wrecks
each what's it called *risk-*
seeking behavior Each
of them a kind of
suicide that we don't
talk about as suicide
because we're NDN
and who's listening Ppl
driving drunk or huffing
paint n glue for the vapors
bc gripping knotted darkness
No way to lift
out of police sirens, knives
and night fights, history
class One paragraph on yr time
with the land—shrinking
dendrites of chronic stress
The impulses slow Tin
foil in windows
When cultural inheritance
is generational trauma,

hunted by governments
by Spain, by Mexico, by the United
States, by pathogens by
black mold in shitty mobile
homes Being sprayed
on like roaches by Cath-
olicism, by crack pipes, by
tweakers, by Chupa Chup
with his shotgun
Mom answers
the door He's hollering
Punkin (my dad) *said he*
was gonna paint my FUCKING
license plate But my dad
fathoming the idea of/being
tribal chairman, is away
on business or a binge
My mom
after her shift
at thrift store at RV
park, perm'd curls, takes
a drag of her cig.
Slow, locked eyes.
Takes the license plate
from Chupa. Sets it on
the linoleum. Paints the
"California" orange or
whatever, never leaving
cig. Hands it back
to him. Says, *Leave.*
In a way that I've
never been able to
argue with Lucky pulls
out a rifle, points
it at me n my dad I duck
behind the dash faster

than my brain can tell me
bc I was taught to do this
I have a machete under the bed
Mom screams at the cop *Let*
her go you red-headed fucker
Someone throws a bottle or
a rock Tony falls back The blunt
force of his trunk on the floor
The knife We pull up to the
scene Bunty still screaming
doesn't know that's *his* trail
of grated skin on the asphalt
Being sprayed
on like roaches by cap-
italism, by metabolic dis-
ease, by team sports names,
mascots, by general invisibility
of being a function of the
past, being a feature
of the land By forced Indian
boarding schools with
20% mortality rates—
By the English fucking
language with its high
beams in my face I'm
totally caught
off guard when Muse
texts me *don't respond*
don't respond don't
respond don't spondee
respond don't respond
Then text five things in a
row and fucking kill myself.
I mean my phone. Delete
Facebook because okay just
because in general just bc

you hate yourself
doesn't mean yr allowed
to be an asshole. Stop
fucking posting about
Klonopin, or cutting yourself,
or throwing up—Save it
for a shitty poem like a normal
wretch. Boundaries
aren't cages. Meter
is a fine flute.
But maybe nobody wants
to hear you. Maybe
you are just an asshole.
I mean, you never
really treat me that
well. We just get com-
fortable with each other
at a time when comfort
something come stop the shaking
is more important than
privacy So I turn my phone
back on, text Michael
He's at work I say *come*
after, he says *going out*
in Chinatown and who fucking
goes out in Chinatown
after midnight on a Thursday?
All I know are boys, boys, boys,
and I hate all of them Stop
fucking posting about how
you want soup, or what's in
your bath water, or what color
are your toenails Just
watch a porn and take a nap
like an adult *sit and scroll*
and fume and sit and scroll

and fume and sit and scroll
and fume and that's—
That's how you catch
the vapors. *Muse...*
music... museum The tune
of memory—The drinking
fountains in Paris
The disappearing fog
Muse, a punk
alcoholic San Francisco
early morning Polaroid
of deep breathing
in a tight sweater Burnt
sienna—inviting oil slick
rainbow A copper jumpsuit
draped on a lampshade Lip-
stick print on a bay
window and the wind-
ow is broken and nobody
is home—Maroon road
rage The way you can't see
stars in the city but we
have street lamps Smudged
yellow leather elbow
patch on a smoking jacket
The brink of eyelashes
The clink of rousing
from a nap Coming to
or coming in or on
8pm and I'm call collecting
I'm collecting
Muse chasing
I'm watching him slip
from one boy
to the next—
He's a British composer,

he makes books in Baltimore,
he's flying me to Lisbon
He's an actor, musician,
packs me into a pop
song He's fucking
my friend—I can't be
in the same room with
him. We're getting coffee.
It's good to see you.
I agree. He's coming
to my bday party
I literally love his
new bf I'm sending
him a DM I just @'d him
added him *thanks*
for the add. He saw my
message but he's not
writing back. These
are all the same
essential
mans. All of these Adams,
all of these Bens n them
Benz and Rolls Royce's
and OJ's and lemonades and
James' and Bacardi's
Stomach acid reflux It
keeps repeating on me
me me me me me me
me me me me me me
meme meme meme
and I know I'm not
supposed to use real
names—Where I'm from,
in the valley I lived in
for thousands of years,
once someone has passed

or pushed or pressed
into the next life that I don't
believe in, their name
is forbidden. Reference them,
but don't use the name bc
it distracts them from
heaven Sullies the peace
they rest in. I don't want to be
a sullier. I'm terrible
in trouble. Flush
at the prospect of being
wrong—but I need a spell,
a cave in the vapors,
a trail. It can't always just
be me, stumbling alone
head first into these bright
things—Lead me back
to the water of belief
Mina, Guadalupe, Geo and Beam,
Stoney, Ricky, Berto,
Dessy, Woody, George,
Lula, Reya, Robin, Bunty
Beebee, Tina, Lucky
Why am I the one left?
Why do I have to know
so many dead? Ppl say Jesus
all the time, and Jesus
Somehow invoking Jesus
proffers a solace, sharp certainty
A get off the couch kinda guilt.
Senators n shit, pundits
n politicians n shit A fiction
to stop the shaking—
Once I have this convo with Jesus
where I confess I can't
take all this living and he

says the same thing. We know
we're doing it slow,
steady, instead of all
at once like ppl w/guts Wine
mouthed and not smoking
so much as sucking the cigs.
We pop it to Beyoncé in his
living room in San Diego, write
raps and record them in his
laundry room Garage
Band We real queen He reads me
Kevin Killian and I read him
Eileen Myles Drink all day
and talk about books until
we pass out Our stars
I mean our heads propped
up in the morning, pick up
where we left off. I meet him
and know *this is the most
special human being on the face
of the planet* Like, he real antidote
We fuck
with boys on Grindr but don't fuck
each other bc what we have is too
pure for our bodies n I understand
I totally literally understand
how having someone like Jesus
can make sex seem profane maybe?
Or like unnecessary? Unmotivated. Jesus
takes steps to cleave himself
from the world Son of America
But I running start
for the headfirst of stars. The vial
is dry, overturned by the bedside
Did I drink all the antidote? Is
there only enough for one of us—

There is a throbbing light, a cursor,
throbbing absence of light
Disappears, comes back, disappears,
comes back, disblinkappears
But leaves for longer
and longer n someday I'm scared
it won't ever come back—no faith
in absence—I'm scared
and their names proffer a
solace Mina n them
Turtle n Rosie
n Pauley n Quick Bird
n Tanny n Pauley Jr.
proffer a kind of power. America
reclines undying I want America
to know who is still dying
for its sins. I want America taken
alive w/ all my names. I have cocks
in my eyes and songs
in my stars and so Yeah,
I fucking hate you
for wanting to die.
And hate myself for thinking
it might be for the best.
There is a barb of feathers
caught in the February
of my throat. It's summer,
I think. The bird
calls in my belly vibrate
to smoke, and snuff.
I want to be normal
enough to fuck. Muse
stops texting,
the B43 hits a pothole
Keeps rum rumming It's
summer, I think, and I hate

nature bc every poem
is like *Poplars* and *Bunch
Grasses* and *Peonies*
and shit, but the East River
is ambling outside my window
like holding hands
with Stevie Nicks:
so beautiful right, but also
deafening, and kinda
scary, and I feel small
online and in real life
bc there's my body
and then there's your body,
and I don't think anybody's
coming over tonight.

● ● ●

Excuse me,
I need to be alone right now
is a bowtie of a phrase—
so cute right, but so
pointless. The rooftop
is a reflex of imagination
in the sense that my
landlord put a latch
on the door, yet
I have faith it's still
up there. Similarly
I turn on all the lights,
open all the faucets,
run the hairdryer, fan,
kettle, Frasier. By NPR,
Syria blares up n thru
the principality of Bush-

wick. By Gchat n only
by Gchat is Muse
in my bedroom. By Cat,
by Jiddy, by Danielle
there is art Which knee-
tap's a thrill like wearing
hairpins A cloud
lit from within And *ugh*
someone in this wreck
unironically says somethin
about being with the
"big dogs" & the voice
is coming from within my body.
By books I'm body beautiful
with the big dogs By
the oracle of meter:
aortic, epiphanic,
epipenic—heartbeat
of the streets and walkways
and freeways and byways
and one ways and bike
ways of the mind
's nimble tug on the
tongue of the page. Memory
would be way less
committed
without the primordial guide-
post of rhythm, cycles
of turning leaves. Just look
at fairweather southern Ca-
lifornia—so pretty right?
But so so dumb. So dumb.
There's no last summer
of yr 20's, first winter
of the rest of yr life. There
is blue marble sky.

This may be the closest
I come to writing
an etiology of mnemonics Wilkes
texts would I ever date
a guy who rides a unicycle?
Not just rides, she says.
Commutes. I see so much
text all day—the door-
way of my memory
has shit typed
in Raleway all over it I
see fonts in my dreams,
oily strings of letters
in the corners of ppls
mouths *Spit it out!*
She sends. *Yay or nay?*
I would have a hard
time introducing him
as my man *Hi, this is*
Terry or Gary or whoever
Hey baby, I think u forgot
yr other wheel
at home?
She's a fiction
writer, finishing
a novel, so spinning
me some yarn is no big
deal. We are each other
's biggest tool of pro-
crastination That vortex
Nasty shapeshifter assuming
more and more alluring
forms Text fistfuls
of words we don't like
and try to avoid: *primitive,*
inspire, denigrate, sem-

inal, hysterical, ancillary
Rage all day abt whether
words are forsaken—
misogyny n racism coded
into casual speak. If a def-
inition runs wild from
the origin of the word,
is it wrong that I wince
at the thought of telling
ppl they "inspire"
me? An insertion. Wd prefer
to say "generative"
Or "refreshing"? Then the whole
damn day is over and I haven't
written a gd thing! Ex-
change email passwords
bc silver we silver We some-
times Sometimes we freeze:
Letters from editors or
employers or exes—
We have no secrets
read this for me plz
but what then is privacy?
I decide not to finger
thru yr drawers when yr not
home n no one will ever know.
Sit alone w/not knowing.

● ● ●

I want to tell you a story. This
is a traditional story,
this story comes our
way from the ancestors.
This story is my story,

the story of summer,
and nine stories tall
grow the dendrical shafts
of preconception. Rooftop
parties r the payday
of summer n I tell Max
Just so you know, when bird
flu comes—chops humanity
to a stump—I'm going
to be great. I hope you'll b
too :-) Tradition is a cage,
like an Edward Curtis pic
of high copper cheekbones—
totemic, fabricated.
Fear cages, feeds sec-
rets. Faith is a privacy, a
thing you don't have to
explain—river of belief
that one is owed
an internal life, a rich
vista of idiosyncrasies
Like looking at windows
and wondering *who's in there*
having sex? I don't want
to set you up for a *racial*
encounter, but NDNs
are reluctant to tell
our stories to strangers.
There is no such thing
as "Indian," but now
there's no turning back.
There's turning over, bounding
out of bed and head-
first into the hammer
of stars. Story is performance,
contextual tradition, language

class—billows like summer.
Dictionary is kind of a blast
of chill air. Language is living
history class, like you n me,
conquest hardwired
into lingua franca—multi-
racial, neighborhoods, parts
of speech, laborious pidgin
Tongues chopped n left writhing
in the proto-memories of a drunk
twentysomething waiting for
the *ascenseur* Fumbling for
the words *sekt und Gauloise Blau?*
at the Kaisers in Mitte Legs red red-
ding Stomp the length of Boca
Chica for *pollo a la plancha por
favor.* Who deserves yr story?
Not all stories. Not *my* story,
my lol truth Not life or live-
lihood or food. Who deserves
this, particular, story, yr, blasting?
My racist ass password
isn't up for public consumption.
Your suicidal threats aren't up
for my Facebook feed.
Answers, like cadence, like slang,
change with audience. Multi-
lingual flexible the reflexive.
They ask *what do Indians use
to treat poison oak?* Mable McKay
takes a drag from her cig on-
stage *Calamine lotion* Takes
a puff of history. I slap myself.
Ppl know when they're being
condescended to in another lang-
uage. Just go to France. We

suspicious We know you ppl
are only interested in the stories we
gift—fair weather, thrill
seeking. Not concern Not
are you well nourished
Not *are you currently suffering*
any chronic illness Not
are you beaten at home Not *how*
many of your relatives killed
themselves. No that would be
too personal. Irresponsible. Out
of the scope of. Too sticky
icky no no. Just convert
to Catholicism then they'll
leave us alone, right?
Just recount the scorpion
trails. *Just tell me about*
lightning baskets. The bird
songs, sing us the bird songs!
Art is not very kidneys.
Your dialysis is not very well
composed. History is way
more important than corn syrup
based diets. Science
is carbon dating ashes
from stolen burial urns Science
is genetic heredity map
Theories of the Bering
Strait—Don't you want to know
where you come from? *Um,*
we come from the Valley
of the Captains No, silly brown
things Where you're Really
from. Now back behind museum
glass—preserved for our children.
Come on. We

are basically doing you a favor.
You don't want your
stories wiped out
when you are.
Internalizing inevitable annihilation,
the brain buffers. Alien
invasion overlord movies
r cute in a Monet way.
I survive seven generations
into a post-apocalyptic America
that started 1492. Maybe
you'll live too? Breathless dash
from this party to catch our
train Ppl fumble for Metrocard
I slide mine in my front pocket
when we leave the roof. Some
of these fools are slow as shit.
I shout over my shoulder *I'm*
catchin this train—If you don't make
it you know where we're meeting
up. See you there! is my lineage.
Don't challenge Muse.
The thing that compels you
to sing? Don't then challenge
it to a singing contest.
Poor, beautiful Thamyris
Singing prodigy, glory
of the cithara, lover of
Hyacinth. Can't you just
see him sashay? Srsly,
who didn't love this Greek
shit as a kid?
So witchy and swishy.
Muse takes his voice away.
Amy Winehouse, too.
Poor, beautiful Amy

Winehouse lost
in the beehive.
Muse is not
don't write it
amused.

● ● ●

I'm scared
of watching movies
under a down comforter
in the summertime,
w/the undercurrent of AC
Being squeezed every now
n again so good
by Muse who breathes
deep, but barely knows me.
Don't fall in love Don't fall
in love Don't fall in love
with Muse, duh! Muse is
embodiment of abstract
concept: Art, dance,
astronomy, drama, heroic
poetry, security, good/god, edible
underwear, pepperoni pizza, Jim
Beam. You touch
his shoulder and he
scoops. Stab. You can't hold
Muse because yr
the side piece. Art is Muse's
main squeeze. It's hard
enough just not being
muserable *I had a*
vision of love You can't
own Muse. Muse pwns

you Surrender implicit
in yr relationship. When Muse
is done, Muse leaves. You
are in a shawl by the fire-
place, rocking alone
again.
It's important to be alone
again.
Just what is so scary abt
the cave? I… I can hear
my heart beating in there
and I don't like it.
In an effort to connect,
fingers will click open
more and more tabs.
People say there are three
Muses or nine some-
times six or eight but
we're friends now,
Imma crack open
the mythology for u—
Really there are four
states of Muse:
Solitude
Intimacy
Anonymity
Reserve
Solitude carries a deck
of cards. Intimacy brought
lube. Anonymity is here
I think. Reserve gives gift
certificates. Obviously.
The influence of Muse
is not unlike *being* under
the influence, the way a poem
is spontaneously drunk

on Robert Graves. The
implications of Muse pop
fizz in all directions: pho-
tography, printing press,
telephone, flash fry, cave etc.
The temple of Muse
is all around you. Don't patron-
ize me, tradition
is a cage Conflict constant The
argument to post will take
more on and more alluring
forms. Muse must be chased!
Vigilance is all that stands btwn
us and a police state *Tell me*
as I switch between lenses—
which is clearer: A… or B. One
more time? *Okay, A… or B.*
I can't ever see
where I stand in the lineage
of art, but I find being alone
maxes out my HP really
makes me kinder: *Gap*
btwn talking to mom vs
talking to mom
Muse used to mean
purpose in being
alone—Muse is romanticized
by the idea of possession and lord
knows I can't live unoccupied.
Information technology tastes
more and more like pink marsh-
mallow Peeps n all my relatives
are diabetic The metaphors
age well Are rent stabilized
Take on new shapes There
is a great flood

in the world of my head
The waves—Now IMHO Muse
grants you the right
not to festoon yr alone
onto the feed. Whatevs, discretion
is alienating Intimacy takes
too damn long And third thing.
I love a good boast
like I love a god good gossip:
I am so good at being Alone.
All I need is my phone.
Subway, elevator, drifting off
in a convo—no one really seems
to notice, occupied by their own
gleaming pod of longing.
I am the captain of my shit,
possessed by the spirit
of Instagram I am omnipotent
on Twitter on Blurb on Vine
Soap boxes on the street corner
of my mind Clear, boosted, boundless
something come stop the shaking
A sun to fly towards iMean
something to do: mimicry
of purpose. The injury
of hunger is: death. The word
of the day is: Gloze.
To explain away.
Glowing gauze glozes the
etc. Weather.com says
Stay inside forever, or
drop dead. We've ads
for you to click. You n me?
It's going to take soooo long
for us to know each other
ten years.

• • •

I huff home from the Ham-
ptons a lil *bunched* inside.
Witnessing luxury makes
me feel like I can't say shit.
Money is very sharp,
very elbows and knees
behind those pinchy cheeks.
In college I meet a Whitney
as in the museum
n I'm like *Whitney like*
Houston? Money is not a-
mused. Life as moments
in between a skipping needle.
They say the key
to appreciating the city
is getting away—I cry
in line at the bank. How
to get away inside: boys,
burgers, booze. Smug American
condemnation of China's media
choke hold following the
Tiananmen Sq. anniversary *How*
can they deny their barbarity?
Really, America?
That's a little too...
writing a poem n only
talking shit on everybody
else Tyler and I are talking
shit on everyone at this party.
Boys are dumb but we keep
entertaining them Music's
too loud but we keep
shouting Buying drinks

is stupid but we keep doing
it. Animal Collective reminds
me of being drunk, before I
was a drunk. Dude says
he's moving to Thailand
keep it light keep it light
keep it light keep it light
Isn't it under martial law?
He blinks, says he has a half
Thai girlfriend and stops
talking to me. Writers
should never be the hero
of their own work.
Be a hero IRL or whatever?
but don't *write* to be a hero—
That shit's disgusting. I
pull Tyler from a burning
building. I am lauded. The End.
I tap Thailand on the shoulder
tap, tap, tap
I hear protestors of the coup
have been using that three
finger salute from the Hunger
Games *keep it light*
keep it light c'mon Teebs
u got this bitch keep it light
I love the Hunger Games,
I'm such a Jena Malone
playing Johanna you know?
Chop, Chop, Chop
I pantomime chopping
into his crotch. If I was
V for Vendetta I would fucking
kill myself, you know?
He looks uncomfortable. I
have an Uncle Chop, I offer

keep it light c'mon Teebs
keep it light you fucking
He drank himself to death.
eeeeeeeeerrrrrrrrrkkkkkkk
Muse buys me a drink I
can't tell if this is a date or
a friend thing? We were
just at a show This guy
sings pretty songs about
his brother going cold
and I know it and well
up when the ballad is abt
snow angels and giving
them halos I think
someone is going to die
Then Muse says *let me buy*
you a drink We're rooftop
drunk-flouncy Hit on some
convo about a snarky
rebuttal of a snarky review
of Patricia Lockwood's new
book, instead of that article
about the refugees in Syria
Seven months in the Crac
des Chevaliers surviving
on cats and dogs Diving
down
A tight cabin over blind
water A plane no one will
claim to have found Yr
last thought before
the gutting panic, before
the sure icy blackness:
I am a garbage
artist Which is my default
well for light banter tbqh

but I'm trying this new
thing called "Don't be so
alienating" I'm giving Muse
this look like *I'm only pre-
tending I don't want
you to kiss me* I'm
withholding, in general.
Surely Muse will want
to kiss me bc I appear
disinterested in kissing.
This is my technique.
Lol so far, so alone. What
the hell do you expect?
Emotional transparency?
What kind of artless
simpleton says what they
truly feel? It's hard
to quote know unquote
what you want. Art-
iculating that is a translation,
and sayin it to someone
who could give it
but might not, is precipice dis-
orientation You are at a rooftop
bar n it makes you
nervous Nearing the edge
is threat of man
overboard. Sometimes threat
and consequence round
like smoke in a black jar
Meaning *Say something, Jerk*
butts up against *Play
the game, Idiot* n the game
is on a checkers board,
missing pieces There's
pawns n dominoes n shit

A Monopoly thimble *Whose*
turn is it? I look into his
baubly eye pits *I got this*
round he says. There's plenty Muse
doesn't know re: me Most
everything about Muse
is something I read on Wiki-
pedia, don't *really* "know."
Not knowing is a privacy.
I ask about Delphi
Read all about Delphi
I put on robes Make me look
Delphic ten minutes b4 mtng up
so I have spontaneous opinions
about the caves Spears
at the ready Very, *So weird we*
love all the same things So
much info is disclosed from
the jump—profile pages,
light Googling, Yet this one
golden nugget Tugging
infection Can't make it
through the cage of my
lips? It's kind of exciting,
having a thing
to hide in the age of knowin
everything all the time *You*
really got a hold on me
I resent you, Muse. How
dare you be the arbiter
of my self worth *Um,*
chill out dude says Jess.
She says to me she says
just give him a freakin
kiss, then *I had to give*
it a try. Whatevs Jess,

that sounds like a movie.
This is real life.
The questions cairn Stones
pile slowly inside Until
silence. Static is the
enemy of decision Which,
consequently, is how
my mother gets kicked out
of that cult in the 60s
Do you believe in Jesus
our lord and savior? *I…
don't know.* Do you believe
our Original *geez* Sin begs
cleansing? *I dunno.* Say
she's too much of a sheep,
send her packin. In this
way the world of ambiguity
has its hospitable cont-
inents But the days Owl
onward. Confront the swirl-
ing panic of Do I live, or
leave—For ppl like us, isn't
this always the question
at the bottom of every
question.
Make a decision to cut
emissions b4 greenhouse
gasses turn us into
Venus. Let's be realistic:
in one scenario, I turn
right, New York is drained
of moisture and combusts.
In another, I turn left
and go to the gym.
Likin a boy, wanting to be public
with that like, bein all *he-ey*

or PDA
is very grave for ppl
like us secrets r quaint.
Privacy is on its last leg.

● ● ●

Leaving yr status
up to the feed, open
to the scroll, who do you
want knowing you r suicidal?
The obvi answer is every-
body, but the whisper
is more
particular.
Ppl lean in.
Who do you really want
spying on you with milk-
shake in Valencia
filter? Who r you trying
not to text talk To see u
flawless on Lake Sebago?
Who deserves
to be bombed
in selfies? What texture
of the grey audience puts
the "firm" in "affirming"?
Hi, sorry, what's the wifi
password? The connection
rate goes up markedly
the more questions you
answer The more apps upon
which u spread yr sex pixels.
Survival and privacy
do not hold hands in times

of conflict, which includes not
having been laid in a minute.
Vibrating rings of a far
flung gas giant. What is lit
from within vs. what's reflecting,
innovative vs. reproducing
bacon vs. *babe, buh baby baby*
baby baby baby bae baby
I want to be
on the brink, learning
note to self: asphyxiation
My brother has a minor
coronary incident. We
talk about being NDN.
Who dic-
tates identity. Blood
quantum is an American
invention whereby the "Indian
problem" solves itself
thru assimilation. *Soooo,*
yr like, half? My date asks.
My brother Johnny
is on the tribal council, says
so many voting members
live off-rez. We have diff
dads, so diff reservations,
but the same nation Rez
like neighborhood n
genocidal legislation.
How much NDN carries
with you if you leave.
My sis is a singin coach,
does Broadway in the 90's We
have diff dads & child-
hoods I meet her in fifth
grade. My date makes a face

like restless leg syndrome.
TBQH I'm so freakin tired
Of hearin abt everyone's maybe
Cherokee great grandma
like, it's past my bedtime.
I touch the walls of her apt
n get the sense of ppl on
the other side—Where I'm
from, in the valley I lived
in for thousands of years,
"neighbors" live further up
the mountain And bc we're
NDN when we say "further up
the mountain" or "behind
the big rocks at the mailbox"
we point with our lips.
To feel a throb of life
on a wall To hear *echoes*
of a TV vs *echoes of nothing*
for miles I crush hard
on NYC. To have new *things*.
I lay facedown on the floor
of her apartment, feel
the bus on the street rum
rummin The buzz She tells
her bodega peeps *This is my half*
brother n auntie gives
this look like *Oh, uh huh.*
I never heard the term half-
brother before Brother says
he's sending tortillas We are
mixed (blood) but full NDN.
I cd see my date says, squinting
half Asian? Tho everyone
can yell I mean tell I'm a fag
Part of me in sharp

relief, a part of me half
hidden. It's very NDN
to watch Ab Fab bc we're
NDN and we're watching Ab
Fab. You aren't very Indian
so when you watch Ab Fab
it isn't very Indian. There
is no such thing as Indian,
but there is an internalized
kingdom of gnashing hands
A dubious relationship
to "facts"—*Is this a date
or an interview?* he asks. This
is the problem dating
on the Internet *I look into a lot
of fires,* I say. So many
wakes The fire pit outside
the tribal hall Cold grey
dust the next day In the
valley I lived in for
thousands of years,
when someone shoves into
the next life, ppl tell
stories for the body
Dance around the casket,
weep and even tell jokes
Stay up all night Dull
eyes at the funeral
tomorrow afternoon.
Problem is, ppl die
so often we never
get to sleep. I sit
by the fire in your mind,
huff rub stoke I am a ghost
I'm down another delta.
You are lost at sea.

Oh...kay. He says. *I'm not
looking for anything super srs
right now.* Shade
your eyes. The sparks
are scattering, as a sentence,
gives you the idea that sparks
continue to scatter A continuous
present like a long exposure
photo—Some things can go on
forever, like looping "You da One"
by Rihanna, or the colonial legacy
called "constant Debbie Downer."
I find other ppl with internalized
gnashing (and have no gods,
dubious of "facts,"
oh and hate nature) n
call them family.
There is no post-colonial
America. Look at the sun,
so blind, or look away
in denial Bunched n bloated
A mulch of bodies
upon which we stack
our lives You know, it's
the prospect of Muse
leaving (threat of freedom)
not Muse coming (threat
of stains) that gets me
on my pen game.

● ● ●

My roommate Jess
is a hollowing singer,
just forks away yr insides

in a way that defies apple
butter. Science is a language
of poetry, like perfume
or music writing or Top Chef—
What notes do you detect?
Ways of translating experience.
We watch a lot of Top
Chef while chomping chicken
fingers. Jess wants to be a poet
n I would literally kill
this whole poem to vibrato
onstage like her—
She writes, and I sing (In
dreams In the shower)
But she's the Singer
and I'm the Poet in our apt
above the chicken slaughter-
house. At some point, our arts
diverge like the continents
Poetry vs *Song* very *Mind* vs *Body*—
why why why the borderlands.
As the universe expands it all
moves slowly away Today
I post a pic of Pangaea
on Insta for #tbt Even geography
is about moving on. Being
thiiiiiis close but sofa so far
from our secret not-secret
desires, suggests a fate
A grouping of stars. But then,
reading think pieces makes
me wanna barf. Our rooms
share a wall. It feels like
a metaphor Or more stark,
like a wall—
Wall like a boor in a bar

Friend of a friend or colleague
n you want to b far,
farther Talkin to the boy
behind the boor
n a piece of u does
go Blank blink
Bye, Felicia
It's summer I think, and feel
more beholden to my body
bc ppl see me in white
tees no hoodie, so I eat
less bread n think more
about dreaming like
almonds Which drain
all the water in CA to grow
in this plastic bag at the
Montrose bodega, but's the only
thing nearing "real" food here.
I wd literally kill this whole poem
to eat like a kid again More
for fun than nourishment No
care connect concern that chili
cheese on frosting on
breaded meat does anything
at all to the body frame
besides the buzz Papa
pickin me up
from school We drive
thru Jack-n-the-Box
bc worms in the commod
oatmeal that arrives on gov't
trucks each month Also,
somethin to do—SoCal grid-
lock is skin-strippingly
boring for a kid Radio blasting
Who has stopped singing Fear

is like a gift that keeps on
giving, but the opposite: series
of horrors that reframe
even the most passing
interactions Dying
is the state of mind Kids
shouting *get off the bus*
Stop singin like a girl
Shavings of my will
to live lol maybe that's all
childhoods Ketchup must've
been a Eureka! moment, like
the discovery of vaccines,
but the opposite A weapon
to never stop eating
Which soda wd u like w/ that?
I get a weird vision His name
is Chad I discover speed.
reading. Gertrude. Stein.
In a poem Sherman Alexie
gives me permission
to leave the reservation I
cut my long hair. Robert laughs
but after school cries to G'ma.
Chad says *Hi!* in the hall.
Oh fuck it's a crush I have
a crush on Chad n Chad's not
gonna wanna fuck my 230 lbs.
Keep slapping my face
in the mirror So run
every morning Drink
gobsa water Swallow
gumball machines of
amphetamines My frame
swirls One morning I go
blind in the shower

for 20 minutes Drink Mad
Dog 20/20 w/white
kids in the suburbs Listen
to riot grrrl records
at Becky's, Mars paints
thick black lines on
my eyelids We smoke weed
at Le Tigre Cut copy our hands
our faces our cheeks
on Merritt's Xerox machine
These dudes slow down,
ask us directions n Eva
says *can I direct yr attn*
to the Smiths? 151
Bucket of rainbow
sherbet n a roll of Sweet
Tarts while footage
of ppl jumping from the
towers flashes on screen
n we sit there Stoney quiet
just not knowing Sai picks
phantom glass from her
heel for weeks Me n Dana
flip thru mags n stare
at Coldstone ads sayin
someday we'll open our
own franchise but really we
just need a freakin sandwich
Cram into the back
of Faith's pick-up w/the
camper shell n titter round
Hillcrest screaming Dizzy
dewy red fishnets the Che,
Lestats, Casbah *Kathleen*
Hanna is right in front
of us WTF The mall the

malls The endless outdoor
stucco palm tree escalator
mall of Southern California
Hip bones but not far enough
from home. Also, wanting Chad.
And William, and Jase, and
Trevor, and Bryan, and Angelo,
and Luis, and Doug, and Brad
and Crushes, crushing None
gay Sad face Whenever anyone
says something *I* don't
understand, I think *shame on me*
and go on like horizon—
largely featureless
in yr eyes. OR learn to say
what does that mean?
Which is an actual Vista,
brewing a conversation
But feels like a hammer
of stars. Google search voice
teachers. I strain to sing,
to hear the bars.

● ● ●

Muse entreats (can I say
entreats w/o sounding like
a fairy?) me *neck w/*
this boy in line at the bar
Smashes our faces to
get her I mean together.
We kiss like sipping
from a goblet I pick
strings of onomatopoeia
from his lips at the California

of our Netflix *Hi I'm Jeff*
We flip
to see whose apt but it's no
contest: I have my place
to myself, but he has A/C
Watch throb
of light leave Muse
and enter Muse.
Throb of light
sprites from Jason to Jeff
Muse. California affects need
4 closure A heavy curtain
Squeezes like a thing
you just live with. The closure
opens unzips to pure We
are in a movie
of my mind We're reaching clima-
te change—Price/point: I pay
for everything: to stand
sit run etc. To hang out wherever
is price of iced coffee etc.
I don't like this etc.
Cough it up. They say
the key to appreciating
the city is getting away.
I cry in line at the bank.
How to get away inside—
boys, burgers, booze.
Wanting to get away is itself
a kind of escape. Bodega sale
on salt & vinegar potato
chips I stand scooped Throb
of light skips from Jeff to
salt & vinegar afternoon. Fucking
in a closet is basically every Hart
Crane poem, yet there's something

to be said about deleting
all Internet wisps of yrself,
Go ham on real life *Being lonely*
gives you a poor sense
of direction Until omg Alex
vibrates the smart phone
of my heart at the backyard bar
Friend of friends n Max
can't find him on FB
or the RSVP list on
the event page and Alex
becomes Muse.
I sit scooped, throb
of light leaves salt & vinegar
into Alex Muse The
very un-IRL mystic
satchel of his Link'd In
n I'm like *fuck reserve*
n I'm like *give me all of*
the knowledge I'll take
the too much of everything—
I'll take shanks
of desert refugees and
Tweets *my sushi brings*
all the boys to the yard
and Pretty Little Liars
and TMI suicide crap
and detox talk and even FB
I'll take it all back into me to
internet stalk the shit outta
this mf. The buffer of wanting
crush to take effect inside
the Crush, this seeding,
is like any dark u prepare
for Like sleep, like knowledge
of death n exes' marriages.

It's agonizing. It keeps
me, the rag & bone ghosts
of my sleep, tense. "Wanting
to be stolen" wraps
me in its fag fingers
on the subway, behind the wheel,
@ signs for eyes
when I should be paying
attention to ballet, musical,
whatever art happens in dark
rooms like womb. Muse,
you can't stare too much
into the sun of his answers.
Friends wave away the idea
of him, like he smells bad.
There's my body,
and then there's yore
body, n somehow you see
a person where I can't
even look long enough
to form a lasting impression. Friend,
yr essential but there's so much
you can't say to me
right now Like:
Distance sucks
when you want his arms
wrapped on yr waist Slack
on yr pillow Under yr
head In the June
of yr dreams Rollers
whooshing up the inside
Rolling feelin, or arms on top
of a mosh pit lolling,
weavin, head over head,
that gently deliver you
to the Muse.

• • •

Sweat snuffs the body
like fly paper like tight
sweater—will not
evaporate. Somehow
this makes us less
shy Knowing
we're both disgusting,
equalizer, like drunk.
I finally say the *c-*
word and you say the *c-*
word. A shared crush
doesn't mean pro-
spect, but it does mean
a kind of privacy,
in the sense that it,
the expanse of it,
occurs only
to the self. Crushing
on Muse is compatible
with the Internet
in the sense that
Internet is comprised
of possibility. Like. Book.
Reading revealing what
I'm "really" thinking.
Muse the prospect does
not computer, I mean
compute, like commuting
on a unicycle,
in the sense
that it's chosen a direction
from which wheels, tracks
branch into reflex

of the imagination—
reverie, a series of
possibilities fill with concrete
It marbles I throw dirt
on his grave n all I want
is to hear him eating
cereal again. The allure
of Muse, is shirk.
Like Adderall—like cheat code
A prayer that something
easy
will emerge, replace the work
required to make love
or art or peace
or thin or smart
or trill or public
health interventions on NDN
reservations. Muse banks
on fantasy, the thrill
of sassing every moment
Like stride through
Neukölln, graffiti parks
of Prenzlaur Berg, huff
the steps of Sacré-Cœur
past the gate chain, the cops,
to the bluffs The bald
part of the park
for the fireworks We
see them miles off
in all directions Speeding
through Cartagena
tempest, V of brown
water like wings Water
slooshing inside when car
door opens Ron Medellin
We clay caked mud volcano

halfway to Barranquilla
Poutine-dizzy we stumblr
back to the Mile End flat
on Blvd Saint Joseph O
with the foam bed
we crash into,
cheek print on the glass
Walking head-first
like babies *carry me*—
We only ever have 1st
conversations. Shoot
the shit. When I say *Muse,*
tell me about yr
family I'm rocking
alone again. Stay insane
sunset on the Seine past
10pm, at the table with
the bottles
in the loud bar
on the Lower East Side.
It doesn't matter
what we say as long as
we laughing, so all
our teeth
earn their keep.
Anytime heavy,
rum rum along—
thus the point of rum
rumming to the city.

● ● ●

Flit is fun
in flit moments,
flick of flick rain tips

on eyelids n such.
Constant flights
of tequila, bawling yawn
Flitting apt to apt,
on n off sidewalks
Shouldering out of ppls way.
Flit Muse every two weeks—
The kick of new Speedy
feeling The unrelenting
city The deathless is wear
and tearing me down.
Have you ever just wanted
to slow? Stop? Settle? This is
incompatible with Muse.
Settling down is Girard.
Girard is what we call
collecting the landmarks,
building up the map
of broken milk trucks
rounding the mountains
of Mexico City The lights
unfold for us, and
pointing to the map at
dinners. Tellin the story
instead of living the story.
This is rent to own. This
is grown. This is feet
planted in a squat
with a kettle bell—
Let the dust
catch up.
Wind marches along
the Hudson. Squint
into a house with
a crib. Paper route.
A lawn n other trappings

of the normal life. TBQH
I find that kinda retch-worthy.
NDN ppl tell time
by funerals, my bro-
ther says. Mom rocks,
nods her head. Brother
plants new trees
in the front yard, something
to do. Likewise I'm happy
to rake leaves. The wind
whips in an unseasonable
chill. For seven days
I chop vegetables, call
my father, wrap
Pendleton blankets around
our legs while watching
Ghost Adventurers, Hoar-
ders, tip-toe our tongues
around the past few
months. Shorter hair. Sighs.
She lines the piano's fell
board. Smiles by the face
of the clock. Warms the
walls by the front
and back doors.
At times, mom stops
talking. Out in the mountains
animal howls in the sky flatten
& diffuse. I forgot silence,
like hands cupped over
ears, huge swath of valleys
of silence, makes its own
skin. I squint
into a trailer, cup hands
around my eyes to see
inside, see a me sitting

with a map I'd made
n tacked up n little relatives
pointing at the pics
all around the walls Dust
swirling on the bullet
roof overhead. They
ask me to tell them
stories, *tell us about bklyn!*
OMG
That was you, Uncle
Teebs? OMG that was
Uncle Teebs!!! OMG
You were so beautiful.
I look down
to my plump
fingers, belly resting
on top of marshmallow
thighs. My vanity never
left, I just got accustomed
to resignation. I talk
dance parties, all
the writers and artists
the musicians, my old
roommates, Muses, lost
loves, the apartments
The shitty shitty apts, *OMG,*
this one time we lived next
to a chicken slaughterhouse—
On the roof, the roaches
brought the rats n the
rats brought feral cats
n the cats brought raccoons
Brooklyn menagerie we
called it Sunsets on the East
River. Sweaty warehouse dance
parties. Pull out a dusty

magazine, a poem
miracle of mine inside. *You*
were a poet Uncle Teebs?
Later, I pull
the peach curtains
closed. Springs groan,
I hit the pillow. I am
alone.
That's also garbage talk.
Future is a delusion, dilute
with reflex of imagination.
I put on rain slicks. The end.

● ● ●

First conversations
are ideal. You can
be anyone
for a few hours.
Once, for a party,
I am Mariah Carey
's back-up singer.
I have this period
of brief
but intense
affairs, for the past
15 years. Lips marble
from sudden heavy
hickeys in the space
between new strangers
But it's better than knowing
it wd rain when he came
home Valley behind the shadow
of the mountain
It's over.

A handing over.
I tell Piano Man
some mates aren't men
meant for bf work.
I tell Baltimore
it's okay you didn't
love me in my love's
season. I tell Big-Arms-
Ugly-Face *I'm with Art Fag.*
I tell Art Fag *I'm with Boyo.*
Boyo tells me a Dire
Straits line *it's just*
that the time
was wrong, Juliet.
I tell Short George
I wrote u a poem and lose it.
I tell Big Ginge *I physically*
can't. take. It. I tell Q-Tip Dick
off, with high tide candor.
Boy Eeyore full Eeyore face
says *I been thinking*
the same thing. As-An-Actor
looks at me, the door,
then back to his TV.
Pompadour says *come*
over, nothing more. Battery
Breath gives me crabs. Baby
Baby Baby says whatever
I tell him. Dimples stops.
Lil Burps puts his hand
in my back pocket
at a record store while
buying Diana Ross
on vinyl but for some
reason I stop…? Jumpy
says *snuggle* and Party Photog

says *cuddle* n I don't traffic
in euphemisms for *fuck*
so, stop. Tall Paul takes
off his socks, and I'm in that
phase where I can't respect
a man after I've seen his feet
so, Stop. Slim Jim, Crazy Karl,
Perfume Guy, Frosted Tips,
Ballet Bottom, Chuckles,
Hardware, Brainy, Munchies,
Herbalife guy, Bar Barfer,
Holey Moley, Scabies Scare,
Steven, etc. ghost, or do I?
Fauxhawk and I stop
w/o telling each other.
That's the best, most victimless.
Pancake Butt and I sit across
the car on the train, don't feel
pressure to say *Hi!*
That's the best. Dreamboat
explains *why* he doesn't
want to see me again.
That's the best b/c as Max
says, there's no incentive
to be a good person, dating
in the city.

• • •

I'm in the city. Am the city.
The rush is what I covet—the
noise of constant motion,
curled in bed on the rez
A sense of options. I'm
starting to (s)well up,

feasting on boys' ideas
and language and chips
of technology. Sometimes
real food. So much is left
to interpretation—the jag
you think is a dagger
as Man says *faggot*
but really says *father*
to someone out of
the range of yr thot process.
This is how shoulders
scoop n stay scooped:
Feeling eyes
upon you, walk to the door.
If walking to the JMZ
summertime and you want
to show your legs—
take Scholes to Lorimer,
cross to the other side
of the park.
If you walk parkside,
men on the benches
will call you faggot,
spit toward you
and sometimes even fo-
llow close behind.
If you take Montrose
to Lorimer, it's almost good
but nearing the turn
is the stretch where men
sit on lawn chairs to watch
the baseball games in
the park and they will
throw bottlecaps, call u
fag if you walk alone. W/
a friend, you will forget

to pay attention. The walk
to Greenpoint is fine
until about Norman. Stay
on the even side,
otherwise you pass the red-
faced Polish men
who will bark at you,
sometimes jut their chins,
make kissy faces
and spit. Cross to Metro-
politan at Lorimer,
or to the side of Graham
to the right of Scholes
and never btwn 3pm and 4
bc you know—*teens.*
When walking with Jess
or Chantal or Wilkes
or Lauren or Maud or Cat
or Tyler or Theresa
or Ruby or Alyson, they
intone walking with *you*
six foot two
feels safer They get less
shit and spit and suck
from men, and while you think
godamn, my faggot ass
makes men hesitant? While
u of course oblige While u
realize this makes you
more that hated man-
thing—this is a safety
exchange. With friends,
u think less about a jeer
and more, *then what'd he say?*
These rules are subject
to change at any

time and you may be
hit or spit on, eye bulging,
broken nose, stabbed,
pounced, and left for dead
Chelsea Clearview rainy day
spit on. Duane Reade
Delancey Lower East Side
spit on. Man
on the subway shouting
Bible verses at you from
across the way, white spittle
in the corners of his mouth.
Feeling eyes upon you,
exploding red,
walk to the next car.
Wipe your face off, bitch.
There is a kind of power
in being reviled
for just *being*
in the sense that my
scooped shoulders, the snake
of my neck, my bare legs
strikes frenzy *I scare them*
Something in the lumen
jolts, terror or desire, hate
so swoll it destabilizes some-
thing about their everyday Some-
thing bubbling, shuddering
under the brushstroke
of stars. The point at which muscle
isn't flexing so much as re-
flecting work. That is not power
I have, but have been
granted. It's more marble
than I can handle,
more ambient fear than I

want swirling in my wake.
Gay bar. Stupid fucking gay
bar. Stupid fucking panic attack
when boy makes eye
contact in the fucking gay feel
of an open, low grassland
surrounded by tall pines,
the neck rolling side
to side—There is surely
something stalking
and knowing
where it comes from
will help the running
away.

● ● ●

It's summer, some-
times, and
Leave. Me. Alone. Muse.

● ● ●

Muse is *finally* giving me
what I want. My hard won
sense of self surrenders thru
the sieve of yr attention every time.
What I mean is for fifteen
years I give all of myself to every
man I meet, mostly bc
I have nothing worth
holding. I want
to get lost, to merge and b
someone else. I look into

the water, a rolling exact
me I promise to find
or make something worth
holding onto. I'm giving
it to you. What I mean
is guard yourself. Erect
fences. Crop a mound
onto the bald land Sing
a Beyoncé song at
karaoke w/yr friends Envision
consequences n make
decisions Loose needles
of light from the dark
tent within Who is "everybody"
in the sentence "Everybody
Hates You"? Open
the book. Find
the song. I flush
at the prospect
of getting to know you
bc one of us will die
first n I develop
a taste for sparkling fizzy
rosé Great big bottles
of incapacitation. I run
hard until dark stars
blast away Tar Sands, Pine Ridge,
Ferguson, the Tea Party, stolen
Nigerian school girls, gay marriage,
Gaza, Kim Kardashian, Tim
Dlugos, fundamentalism, plane
shot from the sky over Ukraine
The bodies in summer sun
rot for days 6'5 white actor
slash personal trainer asks do I feel
connected to the land bc I'm

NDN—I haven't learned to live
with everything yet
much less myself,
so I'm sorry for texting
@ 1:30 in the AM
I meant that for me
Come over, Teebs.
I can't, w/anyone
until I find something
inside worth holding
and guarding and time.
Muse says *Your ideation of me*
is scary bc I'm a con-
struct of your imagination.
I'm afraid when you get
to know me, you won't
like me—Not bc I'm
unlikable, but bc I'm
not you. Lol. Never tell
a secret to a river.

● ● ●

My ex Adam, the first
man, asks what am I
training for Why do I
run 30 miles a week?
Duh, it's bc unless some-
one pulls a gun, I'll
always b bounding away
Straight out of my skin,
back to the Big Bang
Big bangin back into
the dark pocket of Bad
Girls by M.I.A. Literally

no one can catch up to
me *Plus I can eat all*
these ice cream sand-
wiches I produce 30
chipwiches from my bag
and all these ribs. Hardy
Har Har Adam says *You*
can always eat ice cream
sandwiches We are going
to have this argument
again. Adam eats an ice cream
sandwich. I eat alllllllllll
the ice cream sandwiches.
This is basic science. Adam's
body was made by God It's
always looked kinda divine.
My body is a scum bag.
My landlord is a dick.
Adam was never given
peanut butter cups n onion
rings so he wd stop biting
his cousins I mean, there's
no grocery store on the rez.
Adam has an apple
and maybe some juice. Up-
keeping the palace of
Adam is a dream. Taking
out the trash in my shitty
place above the chicken
slaughterhouse n below
another chicken slaughter-
house is defeating. One
morning I roll my ankle Do
I keep going One morning
I want to wake up n trust yr staked
to life, but I keep hearing

yr voice on the phone
just calling to say goodbye
just started a blood bowl,
just lowly passing on
And keep you on the phone
while I call the cops
on the other line and keep
yr body until they bang
on your door. Then blur.
So yeah, I hate you
'for wanting to die
on the Internet, a catapult
not a convo, and IRL
on the beach
planted in the sand
Eyes planted on the line
above the waves,
the waves once named Owl,
sparks of the friend
I love set & settle & dim.
In the posthumous doc-
umentary, he talks about
the future but I know how
he dies. Death says to me
he says *You keep giving me*
all this fear and I don't want it
Mic in hand I shake onstage. Pundits
and politicians wag their grave
intonations. I lift the house
of language, allow doubt
to *whoosh* in. This method
of cooling, antidote for heat
stroke, is my inheritance.
Papa scrawls w/his stick
into the red dirt before
my bus comes in the mornings

We play word games
every day. In this analogy
I am the Earth, my dad
is the ozone layer, and the Sun
is the United States. He
deflects most of the harmful
rays. Me n mama play hot
potato with English—
Quick, name all the words
you know that start with M!!!—
mom, monday, mmmy...butt?
She still likes to tell that one.
Writing is created for accounting
and still does, but is also a
bulging storage space *Fuck*
I'm a hoarder I give my books
away. Pundits and politicians
quiver over immigration.
Humans often followed birds
and herds, and in Hawaii
they planted taro to
stay
alive.
I like to keep trying new
ways of being staked,
which gives me context
to yr outlet, the Internet.
We know wanting to die
isn't the coup in Thailand
and Muse isn't Syria,
or ebola, or Craq
de Chevalier.
At my best
I have the luxury
of speaking for my-
self. *I* becomes

medium. I recoil
at *We*: Now *we*
know; *We* feel love
when; *We* believed
the Earth was flat
until; *We* stir with
heavy feeling bc…
I wipe my muddy feet
on the loveseat of *We*
unless I'm talking
about *you* and *me*.
Kumeyaays knew
a rounded Earth based
on the curve of stars
or didn't, I'll never know.
It's a dark part inside me.
Books are fallible, towers
of letters with the power
you give them. It's heartbreaking
to watch your pillars fall
Watch the crops dry up
and die House set on fire Forced
to dig up yr dead To. Literally.
Dig. Up. The. Old. Graveyard.
n move w/them onto a stone hill
where nothing that grows
can live. Penned in like cattle.
Approaching scientism,
universalism, a supremacy
of any given thought
process—strikes me A
hammer of dark spots. America
never intended for me to live
So the *we* never intended
to include me.
There's my body,

and there's your body
and sometimes it's work to wake
up and convince mine
to stay
alive.
We don't all have to like
the same things—or actually,
fully understand each other—
to appreciate the complication Yr subway
system Yr fiction vs poem Yr egg bagel
on the walk home. My Muse
My love of headphones
bc chatter of the city *faggot*
My chatter from the rez *cousin*
is in the hospital send prayers My
chattering phone keeps me in crush
Keeps me soso in touch with
the latest Beyoncé My lotion
keeps my legs shiny face open
to chatter *and* spit I want magic
bullet But Muse is growing
Sure he is May one day
be prospect And I want parents,
but I know death
and I wanted Poem
to lead me different.
But poems end.
I'm led tight breaths back
to the river of IRL—
Everything piercing
Piercing sips of light
Sober poetry No sun
without shadow No night
without annihilation No morning
without assimilation No
Star to row towards

No myth to speak
for us. Just bodies.
IRL accountability—
Privacy of honest delivery
Privacy policy—
Turning from
Muse
sun of answers
towards audacity of body
Reflection crests towards abstract
concept Gutting panic
Unsure of fumbling
squeezing diff unnamable
this is garbage
god
dess

• • •

I'm loafing
with the great poets
of tomorrow. Fireworks
pop fizz in all directions,
but being in a backyard
surrounded by brownstones
you only get the thunder
and the shudder—war outside
the walls But we've liquor n
Mariah n we're poets,
so we talk about temporal
locations of audio-trauma
and we talk about
margaritas. We blab about
the battle from the backyard.
Language is history—poly-

phony of conquest. So
is absence of language.
Junction. Waiting for the
right word to emerge
out of the pool Little
Mermaid style, hair flip arc
of water—Grandma presses
her forehead, little hand against
the back window of the
government van Her parents
disappear in a cloud of red
dirt—swifted from the rez Stroke
of legislation, to be Civilized.
They cut her hair,
forbid her from speaking
Kumeyaay, forbid heathen
religion Say everything
she knows is wrong profane
She is wrong profane Her
body her face her voice her
language The crinkle
in the corner of her eyes
when kitty chases a dust
bunny. All of it wrong. Kill
the Indian, Save the Man—Sow
a shame so deep it arrives
when I do, it waits for me.
It pours me a drink. Txts
me. One day she stops
eating. One night she steals
an onion from one
of the nuns Tells me it's
the sweetest thing she ever
tasted. She wastes away.
Confounded, the school sends
her home. Boarding schools

are not supposed to have
mortality rates. Grandma survives
a little, but not everything Kumeyaay
is gifted to my dad
for fear it'll be ripped
from him with the same swift
She makes it back but
not everything makes it back
home. I search for it in a poem.
Nona says *you're sick*
and still comin to school?
She looks down into me,
glasses slide halfway
down the bridge of her
nose. She uncaps a mini
vodka bottle. We wait
for the bus. I say I have
a test. *Oh uh huh*
Slides her glasses up.
They rest. She downs the mini
booze, wipes her mouth
with the sleeve of her red
flannel *Nobody comes*
to school for no test. Who
you got a crush on, aaayyy?
My dermatologist sighs *Oh*
what we did to the poor
Native Americans. Now they
got a raw deal She looks into
me for recognition. Chantal
says some white ppl want
racial scolding, n the thot
of that makes me withholding.
Some ppl want scolding.
Others never really seem
to reflect at all Elbow along,

accumulating. I'm
shamed. Suggesting reflexive.
This requires a ton
of voices, attenuation to part-
icular waves of thought. Crash-
Crashing. Crashing. Crash-
Crashing. Crash-Cashing Crash-
Crash-Crashing-Crash-
Crash. What if we just sat here
looked into Owl and didn't hate
ourselves. Looked into the spoonfuls
of light n they shined
back. That's part of the problem,
wanting all that shine. Yr
just getting older. Everyone
does, then doesn't. I'm loaf-
ing with the great poets
of tomorrow, backyard
gazpacho 4th of July style.
There are fireworks but we
keep looking at each other
Which is better than just looking
at ourselves. Can't stop
the latch of my mouth
busted can't stop laughing,
learn to moon-
walk, enjoy fresh
watermelon cilantro margs,
sly swipe for texts from Muse
I'm not getting.
The fireworks start
the building Yesterday I
learned how to moon-
walk. Today I ate
a whole pie for lunch.
I am a pattern maker.

Some lines stop.
Some ppl make strides,
others wait until pain
is life-threatening
before getting the infection
taken care of. Some ppl
pass away. I am nothing
without Muse. Nalini says
moon-
walking is a swiping optical
illusion. I keep falling
over. It's pretty audacious
to take a step b/c yr
always stepping on some-
thing. Moving in a direction
instead of chin-tap calculation.

● ● ●

FEELING whoops Feeling eyes
upon u, cross Lorimer
to the B48 and wait.
Disaster is always right
around the corner. U deserve
a beach day. I miss
Muse more than I want
to be thoughtful. I want
to go to Rippers. Deegs works
at Rippers until Sandy rips
her into the tide, plank
by plank But now Rippers
is back in business. You find
what you look for, snooping
on someone's Instagram. It's
scientific in the sense that studies

are erected within a fathomed
set of parameters and funded
by $$$ that, like humans,
needs to reproduce itself You find
what you look for—Coffee, red
wine, low fat etc. Studies show
benefits. Then studies show
bullshit. This flip flop
is central to the feed This chase
is called watching you presume
new conclusions negate ancient ones.
Belief guillotines down yr
face. I'm lost. You find
what you look for and I'm
lost—the route spirals
like I haven't lived out here
10 years. What I mean is my dad
guides tanks through minefields
after he's drafted into the jungles of
Vietnam He studies the maps all night
Maps of California, the U.S.S.R., the rez
line the hallways of our house—
Geography sewed deep into
me. I see what's ahead and all
around, pulsing dot thru
the Google map of our lives SO
you can imagine how damn hell
ass frustrating it is to be lost
in bklyn Blind particle in a cloud
of interstellar dust Oblong
vapor shape familiar as
a blank face in a dream
steps into the bus, from…?
You've a couple OKC
messages FB Insta
BFF party one time Bar

backyard maybe? Ambient
recognition, like scanning past
the soup on a taco shop
menu But! don't say *Hi*.
There is a golden orbit around
a star where liquid water is keen,
instead of frozen interlocked
or admixed into gases—a
three bears situation.
Similarly, sometimes yr not
looking to get wifed up.
You just want to fuck,
get slapped in the face,
and not hug. But in your
own bed Not w/a total
stranger & somewhat on the regs
And why not—*Let's order*
a pizza? afterward. This golden
orbit is called Tender/Casual/Fun
and not an orbit for everyone.
Nor can everyone occupy the Muse
orbit, or the Mentor orbit, or
the nodding *Hi!* across
the bus and back to yr day
orbit. Then again some
satellites generate heat
from inside, liquid lakes
lay just under the ice,
some extremophiles The
Hidden waves of life
in deep pockets—*No!* This
particular orbit is not hospitable
for life. Feeling eyes upon you,
play candy puzzle app game.
Ignoring each other is merciful
for everyone. On a day like

bright watermelon you take
out the earbuds, say *Hi!*
I think I met you, it was
a party Maybe you're friends
with Danny—I saw yr Tumblr
I oh God was it Grindr sorry
I drink a lot n he says *Actually*
you might know me from
Project Runway Season 5.
Live visibly, is terrifying. Pin-
prick and the air rush
of arctic snuff I will die
of exposure, gasses siphon
into atmosphere admixture My
brother LOVES coming to Times
Square when he visits The rush
of life all around. But living
in the feed grinds u down.
Driver, roll up the partition
is what I call keeping
on yr sunglasses inside.
Saving something for the self.
I can't write poems
the way they must come
to others. Can't use words
like *tamp* or *tincture*, n that
makes me feel like a chump
fraud fool I await rebirth
in the Wayne's World soundtrack.
Hunker into Salt & Vinegar
chips, TLC—The spiral of comfort
leads you in
and out, safely. Every
day is every day
when you *Creep ooh I ooh I*
Tide lets go of the land

as I jump in for a swim—
sandy belly flop. Red chin Thank
god I do everything alone.
The Owl doesn't deign.
I want to scream U R A
HUNGRY PREDATOR
I text Girard. Nothing yet. Nothing
yet Nothing Nothing YET nothing
yet Yet Nothing Yet Arms and legs
kick swirl swish when sleep
finally sets.

● ● ●

I'm done with the moon
It's a phase. I love Leos
I hate grammar. It's grand-
ma. Anyone whose club
who has a club or
I can't say foot I couldn't
be part of—wait. Let's go
clubbing. What? Some nights I
still go out, fading ecological
niche—shook like the sky
in thunder. It's dead
summer, everyone shiny. Lines
for the bar get longer,
lines of my face beating
time, like the sun. Friend of friend
touches my face *You're never*
going to age which means I look
younger than I am but I'm also
like, did she just Thinner-curse
me? Lines
are so industrious, always

going somewhere.
Sleeping alone entombs
me to Netflix n palpitations.
I miss being stone hills I mean
cruised—I am a sweet authentic
person. I was a dream
glowing and shrinking and
growing inside ancestor
survival instincts. I can show
you how the Earth shudders
before it knows it's dead. So…
who do I have to blow to get
some damn sex over here?
I'm saying my land was jam-
med with brawny English,
and I'm still single.
I'm not fond of men-
tioning dreams in poems
or in bars, but I'm Uhura
in a Hunger Games arena.
You are Anaconda-era Ice
Cube and I have a crush
on you. Museless, I'm useless.
I have Grindr and clean
water, once believed in God
and comment boards. Live
a little, says the tarot card
passing out on top of me.
Like balloons, I dreamed
of one day wearing taffeta.
I am dumped for Roy Ayers.
I resurrect to karaoke Tues-
days. I Anthony Kiedis, Janet
Jackson, and never miss
any body. Somethin tall n human
at the lip of the bar. Men

are annoying, refusing to run
in a downpour. I am bellow,
tickle, ellipses. I am hidden
waves of life along the outer
banks of our debate. Giggle
the kernel of pain into
a cry later situation I am
lines in a mirror, smile backwards.
Is it wrong to say I'm bitter
that there's one surviving
native speaker on my Rez?
It's time we swish to water
you say, in a fit of sobriety.
It's hard
to see anything but blood
in the tap, knowing ancestors
died to keep green lawns
over desert sand. It's dead
summer, every lover a river
of sweat in my bed. You
look into the current, wonder
at the bank what ppl *think*.
Strong swirling results. I say
stay, I plead if that's yr thing,
buoyed by pillows by
knees I double back onto you
send yr nerves shooting
like a mind understanding new
terms. *Hold up!* That's the future
piping through that I'm
becoming attuned to. I put
my cheek to the wall I call
out for, invoke if that's yr thing,
Muse goddess take my palm
Muse fuckin tell me I
squeeze my (yoga term) noggin

Let go of paisley freeways,
Let go of jingle dress and basketball
Let Go of train tunnel where some-
thing human colluded is still cooling
Let go of fearing summer's downturn
Let go of significant swells
that write themselves Let Go
of climate control control control
Let go of stone mountains,
remembering the world rounds.
Would that saying were doing,
invoking were curing,
cutting were outing,
I'd have spelled myself home
Spelled the ruptures' sutures
a thousand times by now.

● ● ●

I have a problem
opening my mouth
all the way. The full & res-
onant tone can't escape
until you've opened up
a little bit more. Try yawning.
My singin teacher asks
do I have TMJ. *No, Pam* I say.
I have an athletic mind
with a crushing dominion
over my body NBD Ppl love casting
pathologies. I sing super
high *That's crazy* she says,
U were castrati in another
life No, Pam. In another life
I have hundreds

of horses, ferry Kumeyaay
children to school, men
and women to fiestas
btwn reservations Weave
dry leaves n reeds
n branches into baskets
Loop darker strips into
lightning bolts n the cloud
patterns that roll around
our sacred mountain I live
in the Valley of the Captains
sing Bird, the epic song cycles
that narrate how we got
to the valley and what we passed
on our way Time to time I scout
from the mountain peak, light a fire
in my feet when the Spanish
flood into the vineyards
We retreat into the crevice
of the Earth but the storm,
it never blows
over. At the mission,
I learn to read Grow
food for the priest
Scrub our shackles
for the bible tells me so.
I've never liked church, but I love
midnight mass, love singing lessons
after 8pm, love night writing.
The ceremony of nighttime,
the cauldron of echoes, smells,
the Earth's shadow over itself—
curates an intimate thought
process, a witchy kind
of attention. The sun is
too canine for me. Drooling

and jumping and expects thanks
for just being. Too much *into* everything.
I look up at blinking string lights
crisscrossing the sky *wtf r u DOING*
with yr life? Less
Mary Oliver and more Mary
Magdalene, in that language
is a garden tended by succeeding
generations Flowers watered,
weeds pulled But words
change n rules change How
"hate" was pronounced more
like "hot" Really seething
I mean seeing something adds
to its poetry Then conquerors
invade the narrative n just mow
the whole thing My colonial mind
So that I'm at this party shoutin
over (ugh) dub step abt Mary
Magdalene n historical
revisionism I heard on this
comedy podcast instead of the
changing nature of Frog
in Kumeyaay trickster stories
bc they're gone n I never learned
them Mary in the sense that
u live yr life n after u die, writing
lives on—says whatever
it wants about you. Like
leaving a party alone and
catching the train n rem-
ember every dumb ass thing
u said?
Everyone hates you.
They could help it, but
you can't. You keep shitting.

I look up and fall down
bc the distance btwn Bushwick
and the north star smacks
my equilibrium across the face.
Ppl survive all the time,
thru true horrors Holocaust,
Middle Passage, 1492 like *how?*
I am one of the weak ones.
I cry at Beyoncé songs.
I see a young mom drunk
on the subway Throw up
blueberries or black beans
n her kid son holds her hand,
waves away strap-hangers,
forgets his happy birthday
candle on the seat The doors
close at their stop I cry
for a straight week. The seam
of my skin bursts open
routinely. It's a condition. In
the valley I lived in for
thousands of years, in trad-
itional times, I'm sure I would
have been a mourner, called
on to cry bc I do it all the time.
So I sit on the leg
of my *don't write it* soul
for hours to feel nothing.
Do we deserve privacy
in the age of selfies—pardon
if I *don't say it* muse for
a moment—if we're just giving
it all away? Redacted,
delete status, unlike—Yes,
you always deserve privacy.
In fact, I think you should

have more. Stop fucking
posting about "veggies," truly
America's most disgustingly
perky word, and pics of yr shitty
jewelry tree Just bc you bought
it online one time when u had
a vodka soda with yr Ambien
doesn't mean I want to see it.
Everything is so extra,
it gets hard
to know what to actually
give a fuck about.
It's okay to be alone vs *I'm
gonna die alone* Is Muse good or
bad, is the needless dichotomy
of a foster God—it's hard
to dislodge him, n scraping
away the remnants (they
haven't all winded
or rained away) takes
work—theistic fate jammed
up in my crannies, literal church
imposed onto the foothills
of my landscape whispering
*I know most of you didn't make
it, but it's all a part of God's
plan.* I whisper to myself
Is Muse good or bad? Thinkin
in this way makes me
pardon the expression
want to kill myself. Good/Bad,
Right/Wrong, Binary is
another weapon of the
oppressor Justifies conquest
And is a method to ensure
survivors, if there are any, will

always question their worth
to literally just live.
Today I am smiling
with the great poets
and tomorrow I cry
in line at the bank. Grindr:
Hey man, what's good?
I don't fuckin know. Some
thoughts are all *you.*
Gigi says *this movie
is terrible, duh.* I'm jealous.
I never think
anything is *terrible, duh.*
Take Portland (please)—
Too much *permission,*
I don't really care
to sit with Robert (lol) Lowell,
and I will cross the street
if I see teens—but nothing
is ever *terrible, duh.*
This feels terribly dull. White
cloud in a field. A bomb
goes off somewhere
in the world I'm folding
my bomber jacket with
sweaty August throttling
me, finally convinced the threat
of polar vortex has totes
passed but I'm wrong
so often we're basically BFFs.
Right n me, we've never
really spoken before. Beautiful
alien, lit from all angles,
tells the funny jokes
at parties I crackle,
show off bc sometimes

we're in the same group
at the parties We're smoking
on the deck, music thumps
from the inside.
Right never looks
directly at me.
Right
has a crush on me, right?
I am too intimidating,
Or am I garbage? Right
can't even bother.
I dance big, I résumé,
bend over to pick up a quarter
and once or twice Right
nods, thin lips eking
a sort of semi-smile.
I am entertaining
in this tank top I run
all these miles I'm not
dewy young but
I have scruff kinda.
I am friends with
the coolest girls—
Right, I want mad passionate
constant lava I'll hold
yr hand on water
Nestle chins on chins on chins
Dizzy or just bc
You break like scales
over me I am brave
We are set in Jello,
stuffed into carpets,
fall on top of each other
like snow Gentle
and always a different
body We live through

our bodies, into the force
we started as. Animus.
But you stub cig,
tell another joke
I get a sandwich
at the deli on my
way home.

● ● ●

My singing
teacher says *GO!*:
I stand, hands vined
into each other *but*
is it safer for the voice
to tremolo in Italian
to belt in Mandarin to
clear yr throat in Aramaic?
She blinks. *Forget that!*
Learn how to get out
of your own way—She
plays the scales, sings
them, GO!: I miss the beat
But the mind is so… photo-
synthetic, you know?
She blinks The shine when
someone hears you
but's listenin 2 themself *Think low,*
(if you have to), ver-
tical, light. Then, don't
think at all for God's
sake! I flush like faucets
that don't shut. The struggle
is real on my t-zone. I'm
friends w/all the coolest

girls They know some-
thing I don't. I'm a killer
bc of what's going into
my body n I wonder
if that input, the *don't say*
piranhas of *don't say* biting
self-criticism will ever
change. *That, okay,*
that's cool, Pam says.
Conjure a garden. But
you can't be thought
to sing like Kelly Clark-
son. Since U Been Gone
blasts thru the sound system
at Urban Outfitters where I try
on black jeans in secret
Don't tell anyone I'm at
Urban Outfitters, got it?
They sell "native american"
shit n I've a reputation
Like Narragansett—how
fucking disgusting Naming
a beer after an NDN tribe?
That company is pure scum.
I mean, I'll have a 'Gansett bc
that shit's tasty/cheap but I have
at least the good sense to h8
myself. These black jeans
don't make me feel
like garbage bc I been
running but also I don't feel
anything from the waist
down bc they're lay-
down-to-zip-up tight.
The stars are anxious.
What version of yrself

do you see when you
close yr eyes? New
pants like new glasses
like new haircut u
walk around like a boss
bird-chested for a day or 2
like everything rights,
then always come back
to you. James is hot,
pinches the neck of his tee
Flutters it fast to let air
up into the Man-
hattan of his chest.
Tonight is the 3rd anniversary
of the day Amy Wine-
house died I still
can't look @ pics of her
w/o crying—what gives?
Or rather, what saves?
Jesus saves, or doesn't
Art saves, or doesn't
Money saves, or doesn't
I'm spent *Amy Wine-*
house died? asks James.
I blank blink turn to Boyd. They
the gendered they
smoke lotsa weed so we
talk about consciousness'
flowing thru bodies into new
bodies, impermanence, n
knowin each other 100 yrs ago.
The thing about *they*
is resisting the fallacy of *knowledge,*
a kernel, a mooring "fact"
that "ppl" "need" in order
"to know" "you"—

bouncing off body
into sprightly idea Which I'm
not altogether comfortable
with, existentially, but
discomfort, instability
of terminology, curiosity,
respect, faith, new kinds
of sense A shape forms
around wisps in the darkness,
attracting stars Sits next to you—
These are the currency of
our exchange. It's very
star-flung. In college in
the library I leaf madly
thru this cross-indigenous
anthropological survey
that claims extra-gendered
identities for a smattering of
tribes including mine, n I
wonder about two-spirit
traditional roles How
would it have sounded coming
from my grandma instead
of white anthropologist Sit
swaddled in the bean bag
in the 24-hour reading room
and shake and just Believe.
Whatever Kumeyaay word
for 'they' Catholicism erased
Assimilationist homophobia
A word I'm not attuned to bc
I'm hearing slap cat scream
thump thump party outside
my window I am the window
of my tribe I lift the house
of Goddess I am a new

ward, draining, bleeding out,
Hello, I sit down.

● ● ●

Is this ad relevant to you?
We would like to enhance
your ad watching ex-
perience. Yr a garbage
person if you can't
take a good photo,
is the underlying mess-
age of "gay" "culture"
in Brooklyn The concept
of fame in the United
States I hate
having my picture taken,
I say to this photo-
grapher at this party
bc every damn party
has to b photographed
otherwise it doesn't happen
And bc the parties
are so boring, if ppl
weren't posing
there would b nothing
to do but drink. It's
too loud for convos
n they don't let you dance
in the city. He says *oh*
come on. I say calmly
No. n he asks *is this*
an Indian thing? Like
does a pic steal yr soul
or something?

I want to crumple
him up in the palm
of my hand But I
guess it is a NDN
thing in the sense that
I'm NDN n doing
this thing. Posin for pics
is like not being able
to stare into the sun
for too long but kind of the
opposite—blank black lens
crystallizes the uncertainty
within.
Is this good, or bad
is a sentence in a fight
n I hate confrontation.
Why do I have to take
sides? Switzerland has
the strictest privacy laws
on the planet, and I
have the flyest tank
tops in America. Some-
how I feel good about it.
In Kumeyaay
there's a concept for in-
between. Not knowing
how to smile, how you look
bent over a book Waking
up on either coast
feels the exact same
Sometimes you wake up
not knowing how old
you are n if Johnny
is down the hall in
a robe makin eggs. Future
leaders are *woosh*ed away

from the tribe in a sort of
boreal way to feel
the greater world, stone
hills etc (this is back
in the day).
This in-between
is like gangbusters
for Muse. It's like cat-
nip to Muse It's throb
of light in-between
the 2 of us Just the 2
of us, you n I. I rub Muse
my neck I'm clenching
my jaw for like 20 mins
waiting for this damn
photog to take damn
pic. In-between
Kumeyaay and Brooklyn—
that it has a word,
even if the word is lost
even if the word doesn't exist
even if I'm lyin to you,
is breath tethering Opens throb
of light inside me. I
don't have the option
of keeping my God
alive by keeping her name
secret b/c the word for her
is gone Keeping secrets
is not possible So I give
everything away I'm out
here all alone trying to wad
up enough obsessions
to replace her and with
it, my God I never got to
know her But strangely

sometimes when I'm cry-
laughing at that scene
in Steel Magnolias or
I can't sing the part in
that Beyoncé song at
karaoke where the music
gets all soft and I try
to croon *ooh baby, kiss me*—
Maud has to take
the mic bc the feeling gets
bigger than my voice n
the feeling I think it's her My God
's shadow walking down a hall-
way away but like I said I lost
my voice n don't know
her name Maybe it's
Wa'ashi or Pemu,
says this clairaudient
to me apropos of nothing
But I'll never know 4
sure So I can't call after her
n then I'm like, crying
at a Beyoncé song
r u kidding me Teebs get
it together bitch My dad grows
his hair long Black waves
cascade down his back b/c knives
crop the ceremony of his
mother's hair at the NDN boarding
school I cut mine in mourning
for the old life but I grow
my poems long. A dark
reminder on white pages.
A new ceremony. I grab
the mic back from
Maud Flip for a new song to

flash across the karaoke
screen Fist breath low
n ready James
is finally following me
back on Insta so I take a
somewhat *risque*
selfie send it DM
n right after message
OOOPS! omg I
meant to send that
to someone else gosh
so embarrassed oops!
He responds w/
a pic of his computer
screen His phone #
on it so we
text n he's like
come over n I'm like
do u have A/C he says
Yes n I just straight up
drop the mic
n Leave.

Acknowledgements

Excerpts from this poem have appeared in *Blunderbuss, [PANK]*, *Almost Five Quarterly, Powder Keg, Gabby Journal, Contemporary Verse 2 (CV2), Prelude*, PEN America's Poetry Series, Lambda Literary's Poetry Spotlight, *LitHub* and *Seed Zine*.

Shout out to Birds LLC and editors Sampson & Justin, who helped me make this book way better than the manuscript I first showed them. To the writers who have (patiently, patiently, pa-tient-ly) helped guide & direct me at pivotal points in my writing life: Jennifer Michael Hecht, Pamela Sneed, Ariana Reines, and Alexander Chee. To Jason Koo's workshop at the Brooklyn Poets retreat that kicked *IRL* into life. To Ryan, Tariq, Nick and our shared office space in Greenpoint the summer I wrote this poem. To Roy Pérez, who offered me a room in PDX when I had to get AWAY from the poem. To Tyler, Chantal, Max, Diego, and Jess, who read *IRL* in its infancy and offered me suggestions and support. To Sarah Schulman, who kissed my shoulder and shouted "WOW" the first time I read from *IRL*, and Sam Ross, who first published sections of it in *Blunderbuss*—your belief in this weird ass poem gave me belief as well. To my friends and family, to the birdsong crew, to being Kumeyaay. To gummy candy. To my forever art partner Cat Glennon, and forever (platonic) life partner Lauren Wilkinson.

This book is dedicated to the memory of my grandmother, and all the ancestors who persevered through cultural/literal genocide, land & resource theft, myriad oppressions, repressions, aggressions etc. so that I could be some queer poet in Brooklyn who smells his own belly button way too much.

Tommy "Teebs" Pico is the author of *Nature Poem* (forthcoming 2017 from Tin House Books) and the zine series *Hey, Teebs*. He was the founder and editor in chief of birdsong, an antiracist/queer-positive collective, small press, and zine that published art and writing from 2008-2013. He was a Queer/Art/Mentors inaugural fellow, 2013 Lambda Literary fellow in poetry, and was named one of *Flavorwire*'s "50 Writers You Need to See Read Live." Originally from the Viejas Indian reservation of the Kumeyaay nation, he now lives in Brooklyn and co-curates the reading series Poets With Attitude (PWA) with Morgan Parker.

@heyteebs